The Parables of Jesus

A graphic novel translation

Earnest Graham

OLIVE BRANCH BOOKS

"And Jesus told them many things in parables"(Matthew 13:3)

How do you answer questions of the heart? How do you describe things no one has seen? How do you speak truths too hard to hear? These questions challenged Jesus regularly as he sought to tell people about the nature of God, the Kingdom of Heaven, and the realities of life. And frequently, he would do this by telling stories, *parables* that invite the hearer to think on the deeper truths.

To describe what the "Kingdom of Heaven" is like, Jesus used examples familiar to his listeners in first century Palestine—farmers sowing seeds, weeds and wheat; a mustard seed, yeast, precious items, fishing nets, land owners and bridesmaids with candles. To illustrate what it means to love one's neighbor, he told the story of a Good Samaritan. To show the length that God goes to rescue even one person who has gone astray, he told stories of a lost sheep, a lost coin and a lost son.

These stories transcend time and place, and speak to people in greatly different places in life. The stories Jesus told still engage the heart and seep into the imagination. They still invite us into the mystery and revelation of God and the Kingdom of Heaven, if we have "ears to hear."

I offer the visual retelling of these stories as a meditation on the parables Jesus told. They are not intended to be definitive images of the stories; rather, my hope is that they will inspire you to think of how the parables of Jesus address the questions of our lives and times.

Blessings and peace,

Earnest Graham III

Acknowledgements

I wish to thank the many people who helped bring these stories to life:

My wife **Shirley** for her honesty, insight and companionship along the way.

My son **Evan**, who helps me to see the stories with fresh eyes.

The members of Bible studies at St. Francis in Great Falls VA, St. John's in Suffolk VA, and St. Matthew's in Chesterfield VA, whose wisdom and experiences helped me to hear the parables.

The **Rev. Dr. Keith Emerson** and St. Paul's Episcopal Church in Suffolk, who sponsored the "Parable of the Good Samaritan." They have been dedicated supporters of sharing the good news through Graphic Novel.

Justin Moore and **Olive Branch Books** for making the book accessible and available to the wider community.

And to the many readers who gave valuable feedback on the Bible comic translations as they were developing, one Bible comic at a time.

Dedication

This book is dedicated to my parents, **Earnie and Jeannette**—who offered encouragement and support all of the years I sat hunched over a drawing board, learning to tell stories through art.

Some fell on the road...

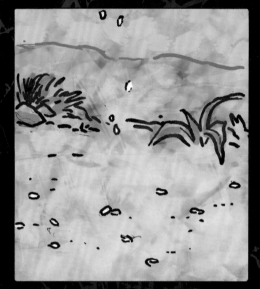

and the birds devoured them.

"Let those who have ears to hear -- listen."

Jesus said... "The **kingdom of heaven** is like a person who has **sown good seed** in his field..."

IT IS GOOD

Later, when the season changed and the plants came up and bore grain

A LAWYER ASKED JESUS, "WHO IS MY NEIGHBOR?" JESUS TOLD THIS STORY

A MAN WENT DOWN FROM JERUSALEM TO JERICHO

ALONG THE WAY SOME ROBBERS ATTACKED HIM.

THEY TOOK HIS POSSESSIONS AND LEFT HIM TO DIE

HE BANDAGED HIS WOUNDS

HE POURED OIL AND WINE ON THEM

THEN HE PUT THE MAN ON HIS OWN DONKEY

TOOK HIM TO AN INN AND TOOK CARE OF HIM.

THE NEXT DAY...

INN KEEPER, HERE ARE TWO SILVER COINS., LOOK AFTER THE MAN.

WHEN I RETURN, I WILL REPAY YOU FOR ANY EXTRA EXPENSES YOU MAY HAVE.

"WHICH OF THESE THREE DO YOU THINK WAS THE NEIGHBOR OF THE MAN WHO WAS ATTACKED BY ROBBERS?" JESUS ASKED.

"THE ONE WHO HAD MERCY ON HIM," SAID THE LAWYER.

"GO AND DO THE SAME," SAID JESUS.

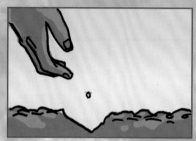

JESUS TOLD THEM
ANOTHER STORY:

**THE KINGDOM
OF HEAVEN
IS LIKE A
MUSTARD SEED**

*...IT IS THE
SMALLEST
OF SEEDS...*

...BUT WHEN
IT GROWS, IT IS
THE GREATEST
OF SHRUBS.

HE TOLD THEM
ANOTHER STORY:

THE KINGDOM
OF HEAVEN
IS LIKE
YEAST...

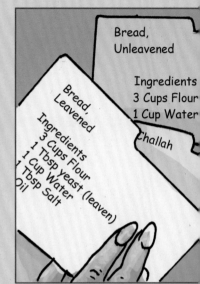

AND WHEN IT WAS MIXED WITH THE FLOUR...

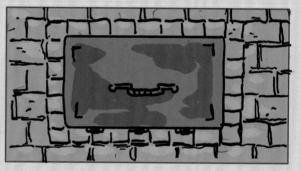

THE WHOLE BREAD WAS LEAVENED.

"THE KINGDOM OF HEAVEN IS LIKE A TREASURE HIDDEN IN A FIELD...

WHICH A MAN,
HAVING FOUND...

COVERED IT UP.

HE GLADLY SELLS
EVERYTHING HE HAS...

"AGAIN, THE KINGDOM OF HEAVEN IS LIKE A MAN,

A MERCHANT...

AND HAVING
FOUND ONE
TRULY GREAT
PEARL...

HE SELLS ALL
THINGS...

AS MUCH AS
HE HAS...

AND HE
BUYS IT."

"AGAIN, THE KINGDOM OF HEAVEN IS LIKE A DRAGNET,

IT GATHERS ALL KINDS OF THINGS...

WHEN THE NET
IS FULL...

THE FISHERMEN DIVIDE THE FISH

THE GOOD THEY PUT INTO BASKETS

AND THEY THROW THE CORRUPT AWAY.

SO IT WILL BE AT THE END OF THE AGE, THE ANGELS WILL GO OUT, AND THEY WILL SEPARATE THE RIGHTEOUS FROM WHAT IS WICKED.

AND WHAT IS WICKED WILL BE CAST AWAY."

The owner went out again at nine o'clock...

YOU ARE STANDING AROUND IDLY, GO AND WORK IN THE VINEYARD.

I WILL PAY YOU WHAT IS RIGHT.

...and again at noon...

...and at three o'clock...

...and around five o'clock...

When evening came...

And so, the ones who came around five o'clock received the full day's pay.

IF THESE LAST ARE BEING PAID A FULL DAY'S WAGE, MAYBE I WILL BE PAID MORE !

A FULL DAY'S PAY.

?

And having received their pay, the first ones complained against the owner of the house.

THESE LAST ONES HAVE ONLY WORKED AN HOUR...

AND YOU HAVE MADE THEM EQUAL TO US, WHO HAVE ENDURED THE BURDEN AND THE HEAT OF THE DAY!

FRIEND, I'M DOING YOU NO WRONG.

WERE YOU NOT PAID THE WAGE WE AGREED UPON?

TAKE WHAT IS YOURS AND GO.

IF I WISH TO GIVE TO THE LAST ONE THE SAME I GIVE TO YOU.

AM I NOT ALLOWED TO DO WHAT I WISH WITH WHAT IS MINE?

OR DO YOU BEGRUDGE ME FOR BEING GOOD?

"Even so, the last ones will be first, and the first ones will be last."

The Wise Builder

The Foolish Builder

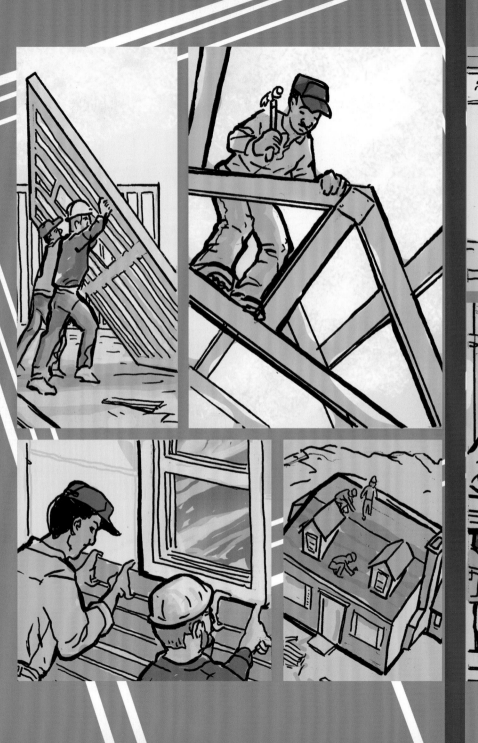

"Whoever hears these words of mine and does them will be like the **The Wise Builder**

...But whoever hears these words of mine and does not do them will be like the foolish builder."

THE KINGDOM OF HEAVEN IS LIKE...

TEN BRIDESMAIDS.

FIVE WERE FOOLISH

AND FIVE WERE WISE.

THE FOOLISH ONES TOOK THEIR LAMPS, BUT DID NOT TAKE OIL WITH THEM.

BUT THE WISE TOOK OIL IN JARS WITH THEIR LAMPS WHEN THEY WENT TO MEET THE BRIDEGROOM.

SO BE ALERT.

YOU DO NOT KNOW THE DAY
OR THE HOUR.

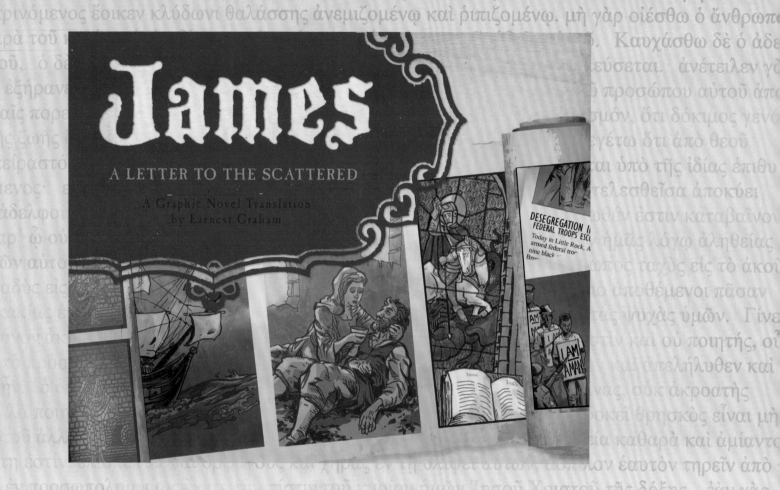